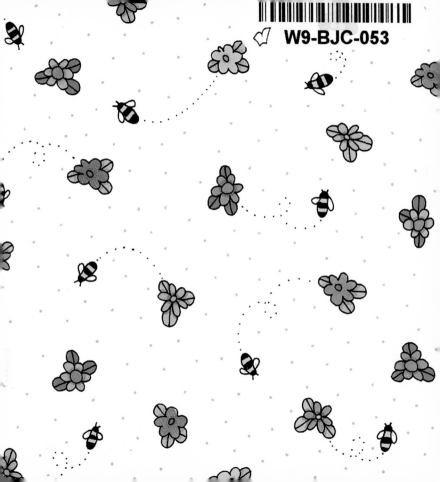

W9-BJC-053

Dear Daughter

Dear Jess,

I Love you,

Mom

- 2000 -

MOM ♥ DAUGHTER

LOVE

LAUGH

FRIENDS ♥ FAMILY

Dear Daughter

Illustrated
by Sue Dreamer

**Andrews McMeel
Publishing**

Kansas City

TRUST ♥ RESPECT

Dear Daughter is a property exclusively licensed through Applejack Licensing International of Manchester, Vermont 05255. For further information call (802) 362-3662.

Illustrations © Sue Dreamer 1999
Courtesy of Applejack Licensing International/Lionheart Books, Ltd.
Design & Compilation © 1999 Lionheart Books, Ltd.

Dear Daughter was produced by Lionheart Books, Ltd.,
5105 Peachtree Industrial Boulevard, Atlanta, Georgia 30341

Designed by Carley Wilson Brown
Edited by Gina Webb

www.andrewsmcmeel.com

ISBN: 0-7407-0089-8

Library of Congress Catalog Card Number: 99-72683

Dear Daughter

Introduction

In the beginning, there was Mom. Telling you to "tie your shoes," warning "don't put that in your mouth." If only life stayed that simple. But since daughters grow up, and life gets more complicated, mothers have to keep watching out for them. As Florida Scott Maxwell said, "No matter how old a mother is, she watches her middle-aged children for signs of improvement." As far as mothers are concerned, daughters always need reassurance, sensible and dependable advice, and reminders to listen to their hearts and follow their dreams.

And then there is how much perfume to wear, how to balance a checking account, how to heed the inner voice of your conscience. . . . Most of the time moms barely get through with one bit of advice before they remember something else; there isn't enough time in a day to tell a daughter everything she needs to know. Sometimes it's easy to forget that our mothers aren't just telling us what to do. That beneath all this information is a desire to protect, to cherish, to make the quality of life the best it can be. Beneath it all is . . . love.

Echoing that loving concern, this collection of lively, inspiring quotes is a perfect gift for mothers and daughters alike, a whimsically illustrated keepsake that celebrates one of our most abiding relationships. As you read through these valuable lessons mothers everywhere teach each day, you will discover something you suspected all along: Mom knows best, and she always has.

Don't be afraid your life will end;

If you really want to be
happy, nobody can stop you.

Sister Mary Tricky

Listen to your own truth, not to what others say is right or wrong. Follow your heart and listen to your own drummer.

Elisabeth Kubler-Ross

Taking joy in life
is a woman's best cosmetic.

Rosalind Russell

The one important thing I have learned over the
years is the difference between taking one's work
seriously and taking one's self seriously. The first is
imperative and the second is disastrous.

Margot Fonteyn

Don't Compromise **YOURSELF**
YOU ARE ALL YOU'VE GOT.

Janis Joplin

Let me listen
to me and not
to them.

Gertrude Stein

There are two
ways of spreading
the light: to be
the candle or the
mirror that
reflects it.
Edith Wharton

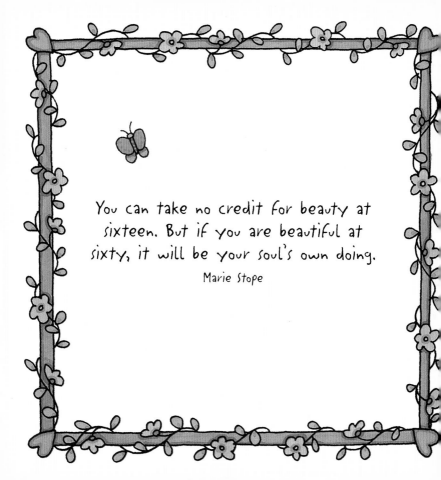

You can take no credit for beauty at sixteen. But if you are beautiful at sixty, it will be your soul's own doing.

Marie Stope

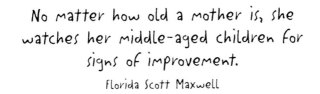

No matter how old a mother is, she watches her middle-aged children for signs of improvement.

Florida Scott Maxwell

Children are
likely to live up
to what you
believe of them.

Lady Bird Johnson

Mistakes are part of the dues one pays for a full life.

Sophia Loren

Sally Berger

Often people attempt to live their lives backwards; they try to have more things, or more money, in order to do more of what they want, so they will be happier. The way it actually works is the reverse. You must first be who you really are, then do what you need to do, in order to have what you want.

Margaret Young

To be one woman,
truly, wholly, is to be
all women. Tend one
garden and you will
birth worlds.

Kate Braverman

Giving, whether it be time, labor, affection, advice, gifts, or whatever, is one of life's greatest pleasures.

Rebecca Russell

Call on God, but row away from the rocks.

Indian Proverb

Woman softens her own troubles
by generously solacing those of others.

Francoise D'Aubegne Maintenon

The little things That make life sweet
Are worth their weight in gold;
They can't be bought at any price
And neither are they sold.

Estelle Waite Hoover

Before you were conceived, I wanted you.
Before you were born, I loved you.
Before you were here an hour, I would die for you.
This is the miracle of life.

Maureen Hawkins

The young do not know enough to be prudent,
and therefore, they attempt the impossible—and
achieve it, generation after generation.

Pearl S. Buck

The best way to keep your children home is to make the home atmosphere pleasant—and let the air out of the tires.

Dorothy Parker

It's easy to pick children whose mothers are good housekeepers; they are usually found in other yards.

Anonymous

Life shrinks or expands
in proportion to one's courage.
Anais Nin

Being powerful is like being a lady. If you have
to tell people that you are, you are not.
Margaret Thatcher

Give truth, and your gift
will be paid in kind,
And honor will honor meet;
And the smile which is sweet
will surely find
A smile that is just as sweet.

Madeline S. Bridges

Comedy is tragedy plus time.

Carol Burnett

I have a simple philosophy: Fill what is empty, Empty what is full, And scratch where it itches.

Alice Roosevelt Longworth

Once a woman has forgiven a man,
she must not reheat his sins for breakfast.

Marlene Dietrich

A woman can do anything, but not everything.
Consequently, the wise woman shares the tasks
and the credit, if any, with family,
friends, and colleagues.

June E. Gabler

Fortunately, psychoanalysis is not the only way to resolve inner conflicts. Life itself remains a very effective therapist.

Karen Horney

Never face facts; if you do
you'll never get up in the morning.

Marlo Thomas

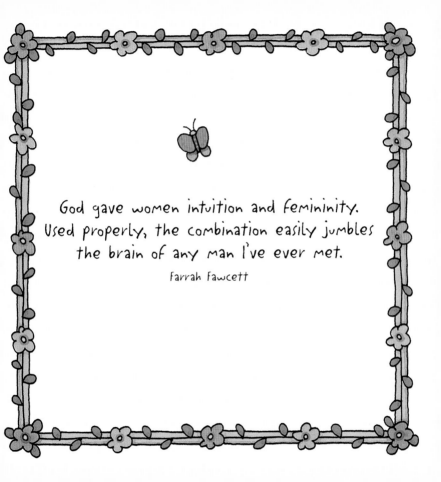

God gave women intuition and femininity.
Used properly, the combination easily jumbles
the brain of any man I've ever met.

Farrah Fawcett

If there is one feeling, above all others, I would implant in a girl, it is self-reliance.

Virginia Penny

What my mother believed
about cooking is that if you worked hard
and prospered, someone else
would do it for you.

Nora Ephron

There are three ways to get something done:
Do it yourself, employ someone, or forbid
your children to do it.

Monta Crane

Amelia Earhart

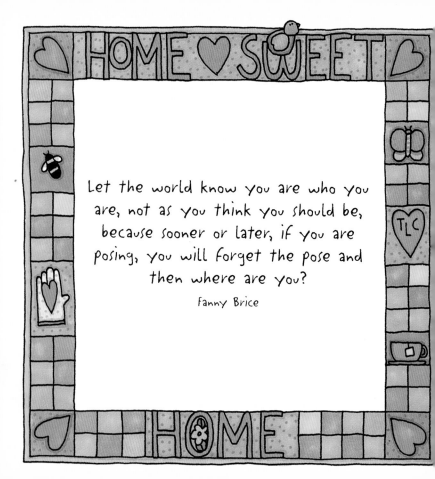

Let the world know you are who you are, not as you think you should be, because sooner or later, if you are posing, you will forget the pose and then where are you?

Fanny Brice

Advice is what we ask for when we already
know the answer but wish we didn't.

Erica Jong

The most courageous act is still to think
for yourself. Aloud.

Coco Chanel

Only she who attempts the absurd
can achieve the impossible.

Sharon Schuster

The modern rule is that every woman must be her own chaperone.

Amy Vanderbilt

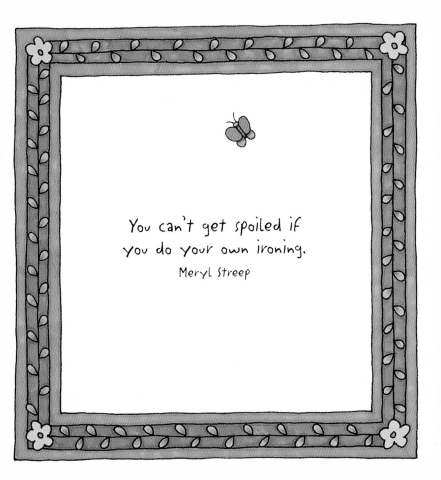

You can't get spoiled if
you do your own ironing.
Meryl Streep

One thing they never tell you about child raising is that for the rest of your life, at the drop of a hat, you are expected to know your child's name and how old he or she is.

Erma Bombeck

Mothers, food, love, and career: the four major guilt groups.
Cathy Guisewite

In your heart, keep one still, secret spot where dreams may go and be sheltered so they may thrive and grow.

Louise Driscoll

Imagination is the highest Kite one can FLY.

Lauren Bacall

When your dreams turn to dust, vacuum.

Anonymous

If the world seems cold to you,
kindle fires to warm it.

Lucy Larcom

There are many little ways to enlarge your child's world. Love of books is the best of all.

Jacqueline Kennedy Onassis

we can do no great things,
only small things with great love.

Mother Teresa